A
star
3 trees
and a venus flytrap

Lara Johnson

ISBN: 978-0-578-33662-6

For Evelyn, my beloved mom

Psychopath
    Punk
        Parasite
            Pissant
                Pipsqueak

1. Bluff
2. Lie
3. Antagonize
4. Intimidate
5. Charm offensive
6. Concede but not with words

Go slow,
Keep your distance,
Draw lines in the sand,
Say back-off
Hold up your hand.

Be yourself. Be cool. Be great.

Be kind and do the right thing. 7:11

Sometimes other people's cruelty is the best thing for you.

People and trees have people and trees who they like and don't like for no reason.

The way to make problems go away is to solve them.

The people who work/have discipline/don't give up will enter the kingdom of God.

Maturity is being conscious of your unconscious acts.

Be vigilant. Don't be led down any roads even if feels like just pulling over for a minute.

Know and focus on your enemy. The rest are followers. Followers follow whomever appears in the lead. When you're nice to the enemy it sends the wrong message to his followers.

A person who gains power by bullying has no real power.

Make a good impression even when yours isn't favorable.

The reward for maturity is inner peace.

Take the day as the day comes.

All acts have a root.

When focus and work don't have time to compete with others. A win-win for everyone!

It's better to not speak about, not pass judgement, stay focused on your goals and dreams.

Laugh is a friendly word.

A big part of being a venus flytrap is knowing bugs are just bugs.

Misery is when it's all beneath you, or you can't apply your skills/talent.

The big thing is what you want to believe or refuse to believe. It takes courage, sturdiness to see the truth.

Jesus spoke in tongues, he did so because it doesn't work to be clear.

Don't answer any questions don't want to just repeat, "it was good" or something similar as if don't hear their prying questions.

Words are bigger than people.

Anything you say to some people becomes their focus because they have no focus.

Funny how humans spend most of their time viewing the world with themselves as focal point and barely know who they are.

When dealing with a monstrous person, you have to change who you are. You have to go slow, shun, create distance.

When confronted with a monster, you have to put on your superhero hat.

If don't want to say truth, be silent. If do want to say truth, in most cases, best to be silent.

Don't give away your power or let it be used for a cause you don't support.

Some people choose to let themselves be used how some use gerbils.

With siblings, let it go. Children are not equipped to know best course of action. Forgive them, forgive yourself.

He goes round and round like on a merry-go-round.

At some point, we all teeter on line of abusing our power.

When you submit to evil forces of cruelty, abuse of power, you've lost your most valuable asset, your kind loving self. When this happens you're on the road to self-destruction.

We make our assessment of a person based on how they look, speak and then we see if their words/actions match who they are, but our fundamental assessment doesn't change.

Once go through the buggy people (eat and spit them out), most back off.

I feel recovered but need to keep walking through this field.

This is what they do –try to find your fault lines.

They aren't going to HR no matter what, and you aren't going to HR no matter what so all sorts of anything can happen but your best card is to not show your cards.

Big thing you want to avoid in life is doing something due to rage as a reaction to pain inflicted on you from actions/words of another person.

Best to be quiet as then as thoughts evolve not tied to anything said previously, not backtracking.

Once you know how to handle a person and do it once, it becomes easy. A person no matter what their master deceitful plan short of poisoning or murdering you, only tricks in bag are emotional ones. The two big ones are fear & guilt and cousin shame. When introduced don't shake their hands.

You can't say out loud too much truth in life. This creates a firestorm. But you can give looks, use silence & have your actions speak.

A person may make a favorable impression in one area but then get to know their dark side.

It seems if you tell a person their behavior is monstrous this has no impact. It seems to fuel the fire. You want to stand clear of monsters. Better to tell/say nothing and keep your distance.

Even if we know our strengths and weaknesses, we are emotional creatures.

Don't move the road blocks to the side for anyone; or do a dance to make them think you may move the road blocks to throw them off, outsmart them, any number of other things which are in your head. Actions are all that matter. They know this. You should know this.

Literature helps you figure out stuff but ultimately if you aren't responsible nothing matters.

If everyone takes a brick out of a wall, there is no wall.

Life is supposed to be a struggle. We don't want to believe so we try denial. But reality is people who accept, go through unique struggle and become mature struggle least in the grand scheme of things.

Having a code of conduct, like theorems in geometry would be helpful for the new world, such as every triangle has 180 degrees. A right triangle has one 90 degree angle and therefore the other two angles have to be 45 degree angles.

You have to eat dirt, be a good actress/actor, put up with a lot of crap to move the ball forward.

People play along as got nothing else or think got nothing else or want nothing else or don't want to work to get something else.

Freedom
dom free
free dom

Godsflow = God, go slow, go with the flow
If believe in God
God is Nature
Nature is Supreme.
Just remember, Godsflow

Fisherman

Man puts fishing rod in water,
If woman is hungry, tired, wants to use man,
flattered to be in his presence, needs money,
wants to escape another situation, career
opportunity, he seems nice, is hot, etc.
She bites,
You don't know what you got until you shut the
door,
Once take the bait, the man knows he's got a
fish,
He then proceeds to be himself: controlling,
abusive, alcoholic, drug user, or caring, loving,
supportive, etc.,
All plays out

In some cases, the man has become so powerful,
in a position of power, he loses sight of reality
and becomes a narcissist,
He also doesn't know what he's got until he
shuts the door,
He also swims in a world where he's the fish,
not the fisherman,
Until there's a world with all fish and no
fishermen, these forces will be at play.

Great Art

To make great art – perfect yourself and then
write, paint, etc.,
Perfect yourself by recording in a notebook your
pain, hurts, and anything else,
Then reread later, type, reread again and again
each time feeling the pain,
What you'll find is it will be painful but you'll
also begin to see not all of the narrative you've
been telling yourself is true,
You told yourself a narrative to get yourself
though the situation at that point in time,
With each rereading you change and you're
growing every day,
You are stronger, more beautiful, less at fault or
not at all than you thought.

Tortoise and the hare

I choose to be the tortoise.
I'm not sure how you go through life if you
don't have a foundation of stories.
To even know your options.
Intimate knowledge of nature, to know it's
beauty, expansiveness and superior design and
efficiency.
Pinocchio, Cinderella, Goldilocks and the Three
Bears, The Little House, Three Little Pigs,
Hansel and Gretel.
I read wheel is only invention not replicated in
nature, but not true,
A walnut, or some other nut, likely inspired the
wheel,
Fairy tales
Little Red Riding Hood, Hans Christian
Anderson's Fairy Tales
Rumpelstiltskin.

A
star
3 trees
and a venus flytrap

A pointing up. This is important and
numeral 3 trees.

A star – a goal, dream, you are the star in
your life

3 trees – entities which bring comfort,
healing and joy

venus flytrap – eat bugs who annoy, try to
take away your self-esteem

The key is to get your star, trees, be a venus
flytrap and then be oblivious to much of what
happens.

Humans are emotional creatures. Humans have
insecurities, even most evil, mean ones want to
be liked, don't want to be shunned, unsure of
what's to come, or how should respond/prepare.
Don't make it easy for them by making them
think you will be nice. You don't have to eat all
bugs, but you have to let it be known you will.
This makes life easier in the long-term. Every
bug you let invade your space stays and
eventually you have bugs crawling all over you.

22

Everyone is a mixture - out of one orifice
may come beautiful music, out of another
definitely comes crap.

Some people have tolerance down, but
may not see you have to eat bugs.

When go to the other side, it's an entirely
different world and there are nuances,
ironies same as on the side where you've
been residing. Funny thing is where you
reside is all in your head.

Tolerance of others begins with viewing
conversations as just conversations. You
have to take good with the bad.

For venus flytrap one nudge of trigger hairs doesn't do anything, two nudges cause trap to close. Nothing else seems to happen after 3rd or 4th nudge. But after 5th nudge, glands lining inside of trap start making digestive enzymes. If a nut or something goes in then 12 hours later the flytrap will spit it out, and smaller insects will not cause the trigger hairs to shut.

Alice in Wonderland, by Lewis Carroll:
Who in the world am I? Ah, that's the
great puzzle. – Alice

You have to be a venus flytrap whether want to
or not.

When encounter a bear and butterfly at the same
time in a forest, which one do you look at first?

If longevity and contribution to planet Earth are
the measure, trees win. Trees outlive humans
and contribute vastly to our mere existence.
They consume water from the ground and
discharge it as oxygen.

Shed people who harvest souls.

Monsters harvest souls.

Every 28 days we shed the entire outer cells of our bodies.

It's best not to let monsters think they have an opening.

Kryptonite = something that can seriously weaken or harm a particular person or thing

A monster's kryptonite is to shun him.

His entire standing is built-on standing on others, making people think others like, respect him.

He's a bully who really only craves attention.

Partly what makes a leader is self-knowledge.

To see your strengths, weaknesses takes humility, discipline

Humility = a modest or low view of one's own importance

"We forfeit three-quarters of ourselves in order to be like other people". –Arthur Schopenhauer

She had an ice cream sandwich
She was whistling Dixie.

There's a pink hue within the clouds.
Now, the pink hue is gone.

The sky was so blue this morning she had to
look twice.

When something isn't acknowledged, it sits out there – waiting to be acknowledged.

Once acknowledged, good or bad, it becomes a thing.

When something is a thing, it can be dealt with and then you move on, move forward.

She doesn't have the fury anymore – in Fury book by Salman Rushdie, it said it comes from despair.

She doesn't have despair.

She moved beyond rage & despair.

At the end of Fury book, the guy transfers his fury to other characters in the book.

The book said we all have fury (rage).

The main character finally loves someone and tries to save her, but it's too late as he left her and she got herself in a bad situation partly due to her perception of his lost love.

The main character was accused by his wife and others of being a person who if you loved him that was your crime, he treated horribly and made you pay.

He was a person who loved you until he didn't – it could happen overnight.

One day he loved you and the next day he was gone.

The sky is pretty.
The rooftops are cool.
Everyone is different.
No two trees are alike.
No one tree is perfect except in its imperfection.

She's grown and come to realize "knowing everything" was a defense mechanism to prevent herself from being hurt by what happens in the world.

Now that she doesn't "know everything", life has been richer, more interesting and she's been pleasantly surprised by others.

It's a beautiful sunny day.

People who play games never make it to the real party as they're stuck in mazes of own design.

She definitely has a strong sense of what's right.

Be kind and do the right thing.

Believe in yourself.

From the book, Villette by Charlotte Bronte: "Deep into some of Madame's secrets I had entered – I know not how; by an intuition or an inspiration which came to me – I know not whence. In the course of living with her, too, I had slowly learned, that, unless with an inferior, she must ever be a rival. She was my rival, heart and soul, though secretly, under the smoothest bearing, and utterly unknown to all save her and myself."

Take it a day at a time
Practice growth, maturity, and forgiveness

She's going to truly forgive and forget and move forward.
It takes hard work to move to the next level.
She'll work hard until she gets there.
There's no sense in rewinding events where she felt betrayed, used.
It's what happens in the workplace, in the world.
To survive you have to forgive and forget, and move forward.
People either live up to your expectations or they don't.
It doesn't mean you can't be friends.
But for a life partner, don't settle.
That's it in a nutshell.

Night Moves, song by Bob Seger & The Silver Bullet Band: " ...I used her, she used me, but neither one cared, we were gettin' our share..."

People use each other sometimes, everyone does knowingly or not,

All you can do is: be pleasant and professional.
You sort of have to know who you are to know how people will use you,
There are some people who use everyone.

Whatever a person's driving force will play out
in all relationships.
-some want charm
-some want worship
-some want respect
-some want power
-some want peace.

If you're having a difficult time in a relationship,
strip it down to its lowest level –friendship.
Some may argue friends are most important, but
we all have a lot of friends. It's the degree of
intimacy, trust that makes a relationship
valuable.

Don't toot your own horn.
People know who's who,
you don't have to tell them.

It's a beautiful day –bright and sunny with snow
on trees.

Meditate
Stay calm
Ignore stupid people
Avoid random comments
Don't read into anything not related to you
Set all free.

She's in a good mood, she emailed him
Desiderata poem and he wrote back: What
does it mean?

She went into his office and said, it means
Believe in Love.

Now she can breathe and relax.
There's nothing so tense anymore.
She's been sweating for a long time and
now everything is better.
She's even more optimistic about her work
and the future of the company.
She should re-read Desiderata poem.
desideratum = something wanted or
needed. Plural is desiderata.
She likes it even more.

She knew there was gold in her mom's
columns – she just didn't know what.

From the book, A decade of Bluemont
News by Evelyn Porterfield Johnson, the
following appeared on December 17, 1970
in weekly "Bluemont Countryside" column
in Loudoun Times-Mirror newspaper:
"Time to gather in the greens, address the
last of the Christmas cards, finish the
baking and rush out again for a few more
gifts. Wanting to catch the glitter of
Tyson's Corner's decorations, we
appreciated the animated dolls and flowing
fountains, then moved on to the lights of
Leesburg and Purcellville but nothing
compared to the beauty of Miss Alley's
lovely tree that shone so brightly right here
in our hometown, Bluemont. Set out about
30 years ago by Jim Scott the seedling was
just about two feet tall, so it has thrived in
our rich Bluemont soil and was kindly
strung with lights by Clyde Beck.
…
I don't believe Sen. Spong would mind my
reprinting a phrase from his Yule message which
he borrowed from the poet Max Ehrmann in his
selection, Desiderata. "Advice for a full life and
my wish to you, Especially do not feign
affection. Neither be cynical about love; for in
the face of all aridity and disenchantment, it is as
perennial as the grass." Merry Christmas!"

Her intuition is her genius, but you have to
be awake, want to see reality or it won't
come through.

"Genius, in truth, means little more than the
faculty of perceiving in an unhabitual way." –
William James

She's learned and grown,
The poem, Desiderata, by Max Ehrmann
speaks to everything she needed to learn
and keep in mind – be on good terms with
everyone, without surrender. Don't
compare yourself with others. Be yourself
– she already knew this.

She's leaving him alone now.

At this point if the wolves eat him, so be it.
She tried to show him the light and he
keeps drinking the kool-aid.

His behavior has nothing to do with her,
he's power hungry.

In Desiderata poem, you are a child of the
universe, no less than the trees and the
stars…

Nothing trumps the Love card,

People can say don't believe, actions don't back up, or any number of things,

Some people want attention, why talk, flirt and seduce.

But question becomes, is getting attention more important than love?

When presented with the Love card –how a person responds tells their character and the whole story.

"Consider everything an experiment". – Sister Corita Kent

If a person accepts and offer is sincere, both people live happily ever after within reason.

If a person rejects, he/she is basically saying don't want your love, don't believe or don't love you.

If a person doesn't accept, he/she has no choice but to set you free or more accurately in some cases you've set yourself free.
Check mate, baby!

40

Once forgive and accept person doesn't
love you, or does but enjoys playing you,
i.e., won't set you free, throw down the
Love card and set yourself free.

She feels better suddenly.
She decided to think through her problems–
rather than think about in an indirect way.

Everyone's reality is conjured in their head and
projected to the world.
The world responds accordingly,
If the world's response is not as you like, ask
yourself, what should I change?

She's truly getting happy, it's over and she's
free.

When someone won't set you free, how do you
set yourself free?

"To forgive is to set a prisoner free and discover
the prisoner was you." – Lewis B. Smedes

Forgiveness, the answer. Forgiveness is the
answer.

There's nothing to forgive, forgive everything.

The great psychologist, philosopher William James wrote we create our own hell in this world. He said we do it "…by habitually fashioning our characters in the wrong way."

Lewis Andrews in his book, "To Thine Own Self Be True" explains how dishonest behavior is at the root of most of our psychological problems. Dr. Andrews writes, "The manipulative part of us is literally assaulting our vital center…." Research conducted at SMU, "…found evidence to suggest the effort required to sustain a false intention places an enormous stress on the body's nervous systems." We literally stir up inner turmoil when we're dishonest. In essence, we punish ourselves. One of the most rewarding things in life is to discover our potential for personal fulfillment, and then grow into it. But we can't do this if we get into dishonest habits. If we're selfish and dishonest, we prevent ourselves from knowing what it feels like to be complete. We can never experience the satisfaction of being authentic human beings. This is the worst punishment of all."

"To be what we are, and to become what we are capable of becoming, is the only end of life." – Robert Louis Stevenson

From her perspective, there's no worse person than someone who attacks others especially when done as sport.

She's shedding people who aren't positive, bore, try to bring down, or harass.

You are only as good as who you are, what you do.

She's more and more each day honoring the little girl in her, and boy was she somebody!

Play dumb.
Next steps?

1 Reality is a hard pill to swallow
2 There are degrees of bad behavior
3 The key is if you learn from your mistakes
4 Maybe he doesn't respect women, in general
5 Each corner leads to a new road

She had a lot of rage last night for about an hour
before she went to sleep, but then she slept,
She's in a better spot today, she dealt with the
pain, it was real and now she's okay.

James-Lange theory. William James said your
nervous system reacts first and then your
emotions follow, i.e. we experience pain in
physical form first.

Game players play games.

It took her a lot of pain and suffering to get to
this single simple truth.

-Boycott lies
-Boycott people who knowingly tell lies
-Boycott people who adhere to people who
knowingly tell lies
Of course, do all boycotting respectfully,
courteously and quietly.

She's learned, be professional, be positive.

It's a lot easier now that she's entered the
promised land.

Some situations are a little annoying, test her
patience, but take in stride.

Today is 333rd day of year. Believe in yourself.

People see what they want to see when they are
ready to see.

The real world is painful, but better than living
in a fantasy world.
She feels renewed,
she's taken herself back.
You grow when you dive-in and reflect.

Lesson learned: No matter what they do, stand
up for yourself but don't lecture.

They only change if want to change, she knows
from experience.

Now she sees clearly this so-called love,
chemistry is not as important as she thought.
It's a nice to have, but there must be more –
mutual respect, admiration and both people want
the same things.

Epictetus: "Look not for any greater harm than this: destroying the trustworthy, self-respecting, well-behaved man within you." "If you want to protect yourself from "fear and guilt" and those are the crucial pincers, the real long-term destroyers of will, you have to get rid of all of your instincts to compromise, to meet people halfway. You have to stand aloof, never give openings for deals, never level with your adversaries. You have to become what Ivan Denisovich called a "slow movin' cagey prisoner."

"For it is within you, both your destruction and your deliverance lie." – Epictetus
"The judge will do some things to you which are thought to be terrifying; but how can he stop you from taking the punishment he threatened? You have a right to make them hurt you, and they don't like to do that." –The Enchiridion by Epictetus

She feels better, she's free.

Conquer guilt, conquer fear.
Stay positive and see what happens.
The coolest people…
This new world is nice: wake-up, coast, do what
have to do, deal with who/what have to in a
casual way.

She wants peace so do her job and refrain from
saying anything negative.

When reach evolution/maturity, you forget what
people say the minute they say it, you only keep
in your head what you want to remember.

As long as you're prepared for what may come,
doing work, right thing, reflecting, growing,
making a contribution, pleasant, not engaging in
game playing, this is all you can do. The rest is
out of your control.

A seducer plays on your insecurities and your thinking that you're special. That's how seduce—treat you like you're special. They let you talk and listen until they see how you want to be appreciated.

You want to believe, so you do and then feel indebted to them for seeing what noone else saw before but it's all a game. Once you've drunk the kool-aid one time, it becomes like a drug and harder to not take a sip the next time.They work very hard at flattering you, seeing what works, whatever it takes to get you to take the first sip.

She realized her natural instinct is kindness and some people tried to use for their benefit.

No one cares if you're attractive, especially at her age–they aren't annoyed, offended, made to feel inferior–they don't care,

The ones who dislike you, aren't neutral to you, have a reason (an agenda), i.e., see you as a threat to their success, want to distract others from/hide their incompetence, etc. They will go along with whatever you want to believe to manipulate you for their own personal gain.

The key is to get your ego under control.

There's no perfect person.
Since you aren't going to meet a perfect person,
you should be cordial with everyone.
Weak people follow whomever is in charge.
Be pleasant, be cordial, but take note, some
people are spies for the enemy.
And some go into the enemy camp,
unconsciously, unknowingly.

You've reached the promised land when you can afford to be oblivious and not kowtow to anyone.

She's traveled far and wide, done and said some dumb things, made mistakes, allowed others to run her down, make her feel guilty, didn't believe in herself enough to realize her value, and let others use her caring nature for their own benefit.

From the book, Barbarian Days by William Finnegan: "Life is a comedy to those who think and a tragedy for those who feel."— Horace Walpole

Fortunately she's made no critical errors and hasn't lost anything truly valuable, i.e, herself.

"What a long, strange trip it's been." –Truckin' song by the Grateful Dead

It was very telling in crossroads dream from a long time ago, when she said "if it's not going to work out with my true love, then how in the world am I going to be happy?"

Happiness is more important than love.

There are a lot of good people around – neon
sign on the side of a building in Bergen, Norway

Other people are like boats passing in the same
body of water.

People reap what they sow.

You will find what you're looking for.

Life is a set of waves to be surfed.